World's WEIRDEST REPTILES

by Tom Jackson

Illustrated by Paul Collicutt

HUNGRY TOMATO™

Thanks to the creative team:
Senior Editor: Alice Peebles
Fact checking: Tim Harris
Designer: www.mayermedia.co.uk

First published in Great Britain in 2018
by Hungry Tomato Ltd
PO Box 181
Edenbridge
Kent, TN8 9DP
Copyright © 2018 Hungry Tomato Ltd

A CIP catalogue record for this book is
available from the British Library.
ISBN 978-1-912108-86-2

Printed and bound in China

Discover more at
www.hungrytomato.com

CONTENTS

WEIRD REPTILES

Many reptiles are smart, sneaky, fierce and deadly but some are just plain weird. To us, their strange bodies and odd behaviour might look funny, baffling or even disgusting, but the weird way of life for these reptiles is a matter of life and death. For example, the softshell turtles, with their funny-looking snouts and bulging eyes, have given up their hard armour. Why is that a good idea? The horned lizard bleeds on purpose, the frilled lizard tries really hard to get noticed by its predators, and the ajolote mole lizard only has two legs. What is going on?

The Malayan softshell turtle gives a fatal chomp with its crushing jaws.

Gharials have extra-slender, many-toothed jaws for snapping up fish.

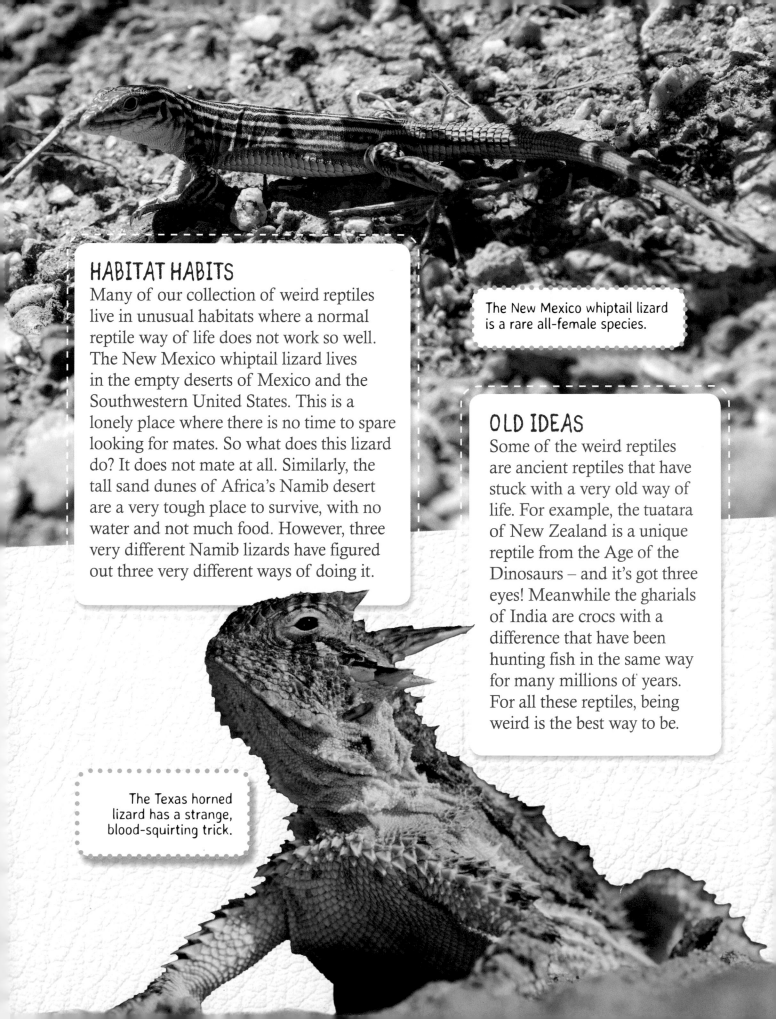

HABITAT HABITS

Many of our collection of weird reptiles live in unusual habitats where a normal reptile way of life does not work so well. The New Mexico whiptail lizard lives in the empty deserts of Mexico and the Southwestern United States. This is a lonely place where there is no time to spare looking for mates. So what does this lizard do? It does not mate at all. Similarly, the tall sand dunes of Africa's Namib desert are a very tough place to survive, with no water and not much food. However, three very different Namib lizards have figured out three very different ways of doing it.

The New Mexico whiptail lizard is a rare all-female species.

OLD IDEAS

Some of the weird reptiles are ancient reptiles that have stuck with a very old way of life. For example, the tuatara of New Zealand is a unique reptile from the Age of the Dinosaurs – and it's got three eyes! Meanwhile the gharials of India are crocs with a difference that have been hunting fish in the same way for many millions of years. For all these reptiles, being weird is the best way to be.

The Texas horned lizard has a strange, blood-squirting trick.

CLOAKING DEVICE

Frilled lizards hunt for insects and other creepy-crawlies. They rely on their colouring to stay hidden. The lizards in woodland areas are silvery-grey to match the bark, while the ones that live in more open scrublands are more yellow to blend in with the sandy ground.

If a threat gets too close, the frilled lizard has a series of defence tactics to halt the predator. First it opens the frill. When unfolded, this makes its head look suddenly much larger. The lizard also opens its big mouth wide, flashing its bright yellow (or pink) gums — and hisses. These rapid changes make the predator pause.

The lizard has bought enough time to escape. It turns around, stands up on its back legs and makes a run for it — to the nearest tree.

The frill makes the escaping lizard easy to see. But as it runs up the tree, it folds down its frill and blends into the surroundings, disappearing from view.

FRILLED LIZARD

The frilled lizard from northern Australia and New Guinea is one of the world's most unusual-looking lizards. At first glance, it looks more or less the same as other large lizards – it has a big mouth, scaly body and a long tail. However, the lizard has a frill of loose skin around its neck. This is normally folded over its shoulders and helps to blur its lizard shape and keep it hidden. However, when threatened, the lizard unfurls the skin frill in one of the animal kingdom's most outlandish defence tricks.

FRILLED LIZARD
CHLAMYDOSAURUS KINGII
Lifespan: 10 years
Size: 85 cm (33 in)

EGG GUARD
Frilled lizards are especially aggressive when protecting their eggs. They lay eggs on a patch of bare earth in a sunny spot, so the sunshine keeps them warm.

HIDDEN PERCH
During the dry season, frilled lizards retreat to the trees and hide out for weeks until the rains return. Any extra moisture means there will be more insect food for them to catch.

MINI MONSTER

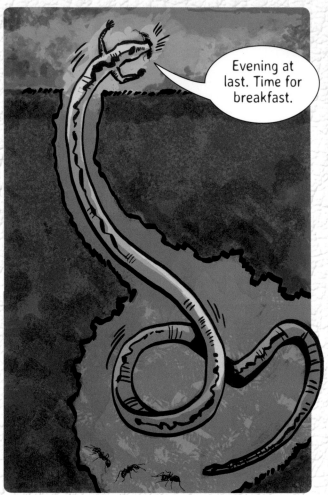

If disturbed by a predator such as a snake, the ajolote starts to coil itself in knots, hiding its head among the coils. This really confuses the predator.

The ajolote spends the day underground. At night or after heavy rain, it digs its way to the surface and grabs prey. It pulls its meal underground before feeding.

The ajolote is a member of a group of reptiles called the amphisbaenia. This name means 'goes both ways' because it is difficult to figure out which end is the head and which is the tail.

Legless lizards, such as slow-worms, look a lot like snakes. However, there is one easy way — although it's risky — to tell them apart. Legless lizards have eyelids but snakes never do. If the long, legless reptile winks at you, it is a lizard. A snake cannot blink — it just stares.

AJOLOTE

Is it a worm? Is it a snake? Some kind of wacky newt? Actually, the ajolote (pronounced ah-hoh-lo-tee) is a reptile that lives underground in Mexico's deserts, eating ants and other insects. It is also called the Mexican mole lizard because it burrows through sandy soil, using its short, spade-shaped front legs. The weird thing is that it does not have any back legs, just a long, pink body that stretches and squeezes to help it shuffle through tunnels like a big reptilian worm.

AJOLOTE
BIPES BIPORUS
Lifespan: 3 years
Size: 24 cm (9.45 in)

SKIN EAR
An ajolote's inner ear (the part inside the head) is connected to a fold of skin on the throat which picks up sounds coming through the soil.

SMALL FAMILY
Female ajolotes only lay a couple of eggs at a time. The eggs develop in a burrow for a couple of months before hatching out.

LIVING FOSSIL

The skull and teeth of reptiles show scientists how they are related. These features reveal that lizards and snakes are closely related to each other, but the tuatara is not.

The tuatara feeds on weta. These are chubby crickets that are the world's heaviest insects — they weigh as much as a small bird. (As well as the tuatara, New Zealand is full of weird creatures.)

One of the tuatara's long-dead relatives was the pleurosaur. This reptile was about twice as long as the tuatara and lived in water. It swam around by wiggling its body like a snake. The tuatara is also a good swimmer, and has webbed feet that help it paddle.

Tuatara only start laying eggs at about 15 years old. It takes more than a year for baby tuatara to hatch. Rats can destroy a lot of the eggs in that time.

Baby tuatara have three eyes. A hole in the top of their head has a see-through scale that lets light into the brain. Skin covers it when the reptile gets older.

TUATARA

The tuatara is one of the rarest reptiles on Earth – and probably the weirdest. It looks a lot like a big lizard, although it is not a lizard – or a snake, or a crocodile, and of course it's not a tortoise. The tuatara is in fact the last surviving member of a group of reptiles that evolved around the same time as the dinosaurs. Today, this strange reptile survives only on a few tiny islands along the coast of New Zealand – and it could soon be extinct without help from people.

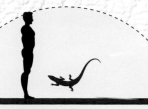

TUATARA
SPHENODON PUNCTATUS
Lifespan: 100 years
Size: 80 cm (31 in)

NATIVE NAME
The name tuatara means 'spiny back' in Maori, the language spoken by the first people to live in New Zealand. The plural of tuatara is tuatara.

FIGHT STYLE
When male tuatara clash over mates, they lift the crest of spikes on their backs, puff up their bodies and darken their skin. The most impressive display wins.

TOUGH TEETH
The tuatara's teeth are made of bone. They never fall out, but once they have worn away, the reptile cannot grow new ones.

ALL FEMALE

Two female whiptails wrestle to produce eggs. One lizard bites the other, which stimulates the second one to produce eggs. These hatch two months later.

After laying her eggs, each lizard then takes a turn as a non-laying 'biter' to help another lizard produce her own eggs.

The New Mexico whiptail is probably a hybrid created when two lizards of different species had babies. The parent species were the little striped whiptail and western whiptail of North America. Both have males and females, but together they could only produce female babies and these became a new all-female species.

Flowerpot snakes are also all-female reptiles. They were originally from India but earned their name from being spread all over the world in the pots of exotic flowers. The snake is completely blind and lives like a worm burrowing through soil. That makes it hard for the snakes to find mates — so they don't bother. The flowerpot snake just lays eggs or gives birth to babies, depending on how much food there is.

NEW MEXICO WHIPTAIL LIZARD

Normally, a male and a female reptile need to pair up before the female can produce eggs or give birth to babies. However, a few weird reptiles, such as the New Mexico whiptail lizard, make babies without this stage. The females just lay eggs without any help – they don't need the males, and so their species simply do not have any! Being able to reproduce like this has its advantages: There is no need to waste time looking for a male to mate with, and one female can fill an entire area with new baby lizards all by herself.

NEW MEXICO WHIPTAIL
CNEMIDOPHORUS NEOMEXICANUS
Lifespan: 6 years
Size: 23 cm (9 in)

BEES BUT NOT THE BIRDS
Reproducing without males is called parthenogenesis. Many species of insect, such as bees, do it, but it is very rare among larger animals. Some fish and newts, as well as reptiles, can do it, but it is never seen in birds or mammals.

CLONES
All babies without fathers are clones of the mother, which means they have exactly the same genes. Having two parents mixes up the genes and makes every baby unique.

Desert Devil

I also sway back and forth a little, as if I'm being blown by the breeze.

I have to eat lots of them — not much goodness in one ant.

The thorny devil lives among spiky grasses. Its body looks like the dried leaves that cover the ground. To help its disguise, the thorny devil moves very slowly.

The lizard eats almost nothing but ants and termites. It creeps over to a nest and licks up insects one by one. It can eat nearly 1,000 in one go.

That looks nasty. I'm not feeling very hungry now.

I'm keeping my head down.

If attacked, the lizard is too small to run. It does not need to. It has a false head! It tucks its real head safely between its legs and shows off a large, spiked lump on its neck that looks like a head. If a predator bites the wrong head, the lizard will not die — and the attacker is often put off by the spiked meal.

This is amazing, it all works by itself.

Can you just explain it to me again?

The thorny devil's weird skin is not just for defence. It is also used for drinking! There are tiny channels between the scales. The channels suck water from the body and move it along to the lizard's mouth, creating a life-giving trickle. The water may be from dew that forms on all the spikes, or the lizard stands on wet ground and the liquid travels up the skin to the mouth.

THORNY DEVIL

The red deserts of Australia have little devils creeping around. With its spiked armour, the thorny devil looks like a terrifying monster – only it could easily perch on the back of your hand. Those spikes are just one of many clever features that these weird little beasts use to keep predators away and stay alive in their dry habitat. For example, their home may be dry but it does get chilly. When it does, the little lizards darken to absorb more heat, and then become paler when the hot weather returns.

THORNY DEVIL
MOLOCH HORRIDUS
Lifespan: 20 years
Size: 11 cm (4.3 in)

SOFT SPIKES
Although they look prickly, the lizard's thorns are not stiff, so they are not as sharp as they appear. However, this funny-shaped lizard is still hard to swallow.

FALLEN ANGEL
The lizard's scientific name comes from Moloch, a demon that was said to rule the Middle East in ancient times – where it ate children!

Blood Squirter

The horned lizard lives in a burrow close to several nests of harvester ants. These big ants are its favourite food. It feeds in the cooler parts of the day — or when the ants are especially busy — and does its best to stay out of sight. Its wide, flat body blends in with the dusty ground, as it steadily licks up its food.

When the lizard senses danger, such as an approaching coyote, it needs to make itself look fiercer than it really is. It takes big gulps of air to puff up its body, making it look bigger and tougher.

The coyote is not put off by the round, bloated lizard. As the predator gets nearer, the lizard stands tall on its legs, hoping to scare off the attacker.

The lizard finally squirts a jet of blood from its eye straight at the attacker. It can fire blood about 1.5 m (5 ft) and pump out a third of its supply in one go.

The blood has a bad smell and taste, and the lizard is splashed with it, making it look less appetizing, The predator has blood in its mouth and eyes, too.

HORNED LIZARD

When is a toad not a toad? When it's a Texas horned lizard, of course. This little lizard from the deserts of Texas can make itself so round and bloated that it looks like a small frog or toad. That is just one of the cunning tricks the horned lizard uses to stay safe. Its drab colouring and small size is enough to keep it hidden among the rocks as it scuttles about looking for food. But if a predator does come in for the kill, the horned lizard spills blood to stay alive.

HORNED LIZARD
PHRYNOSOMA CORNUTUM
Lifespan: 8 years
Size: 11 cm (4.3 in)

PROTECTED SPECIES
Despite being a rough, tough little critter, the Texas horned lizard needs protection from extinction. Pesticide chemicals used by farmers are killing the ants that the lizard eats.

BORROWING BURROWS
The lizard often takes over a burrow left by another animal, such as a gopher. It can also dig its own, using its wide snout as a shovel.

SEA LIZARD

While smaller iguanas feed on seaweeds exposed at low tide, the bigger lizards dive down below the water to get at more food. They prefer to graze on short green algae.

A big iguana can stay underwater for almost an hour on one breath. However, they normally stay under for a few minutes before using their flat tails to swim back to the surface.

After feeding in cold water, the lizards need to warm up fast. Their skin turns very dark when it is wet, and this helps to absorb the sun's heat faster.

Once warmed up, the iguanas' skin becomes paler. The lizards stand more upright to avoid being baked too much by the hot sunshine.

The iguana's food is very salty, and the lizard has to clear out a lot of salt from its body. It uses glands on its snout to squirt out salty water in big sneezes.

The males are twice as big as the females. When there is not much food around, the bigger iguanas can shrink by one tenth of their size to save energy.

MARINE IGUANA

The Galápagos Islands in the Pacific Ocean are home to some amazing animals. The most famous is the giant tortoise, but the weirdest is the marine iguana. This chunky reptile is the only lizard that gets its food from the sea. It leads a simple life of swimming and resting, followed by some more swimming and another rest. Most lizards like to be alone, but this species is again unusual in that they live together in colonies of 50 or more along the rugged, rocky shoreline.

MARINE IGUANA
AMBLYRHYNCHUS CRISTATUS
Lifespan: 60 years
Size: 75 cm (30 in)

CLEANING UP
Smaller lava lizards and insect-eating birds crowd around the big iguanas as they sunbathe. The visitors feast on the flies that land on the iguanas' salty skin.

EATING POO
The iguanas need bacteria in their stomachs to digest the seaweed they eat. Young lizards eat the adults' poo to make sure they have the right kind of tummy bugs.

FISH SLASHER

Although it is not nearly as heavy as the saltwater crocodile (the biggest reptile in the world), the gharial can grow a little longer thanks to its super-long snout and slender swimming tail.

Gharials sunbathe and lay their eggs on sandbanks in the middle of big rivers. In recent years, the sandbanks have been removed to make way for riverboats, so the gharial has become very rare.

Another name for the gharial is the fish-eating crocodile, because its long, teeth-filled snout is ideal for snatching slippery fish from the water.

Male gharials are larger than the females, and they also have a hollow lump, or bulb, on the tip of their snout, where the nostrils are located.

Males use their nose bulb to blow bubbles and send deep, buzzing calls underwater. They also slap the water with their mouths to signal to mates.

Gharial eggs hatch when the river is low. The babies are only about 18 cm (7 in) long and stay close to their parents until the river rises a few months later.

GHARIAL

Not all crocodiles are robust killers. The gharial, which lives in India's wide, shallow rivers, is a slender and graceful killer instead. This long reptile, with its short legs and boat-shaped body, swims effortlessly in the muddy river water. On land it is another story. The legs are too puny to lift the body, so the animal has to shuffle around on its belly. However, what it lacks in strength it makes up for in other ways: the gharial's narrow snout has more than 100 long, gnarly teeth.

GHARIAL
GAVIALIS GANGETICUS
Lifespan: 30 years
Size: 6.5 m (21 ft)

SPELLING MISTAKE
The name gharial comes from an Indian word for a jar. The animal is sometimes called a gavial as well. This is due to a spelling mistake someone made centuries ago.

PRECIOUS
The gharial is one of the rarest reptiles in the world. There are probably fewer than 300 left in the wild.

TOUGH SOFTIE

The softshell turtle's carapace, or upper shell, does not have the hard plates that make other turtle and tortoise shells so tough and heavy.

Although the shell is rubbery and flexible, it still offers plenty of protection. The softshell can fold its long neck right back under the shell to protect its head. It looks weird but it works.

Softshells live in muddy water where they can become completely invisible as they sink below the surface. They crawl around on the bottom or just sit and wait until it is time to feed. If they need to breathe air, they only have to poke their flexible nostrils above the water.

As with all turtles, softshells do not have teeth but they do have a razor-sharp beak that can deliver deep bites. Because softshells are so well-hidden, they can bite fast and without warning.

The turtle grabs prey by extending its long neck at lightning speed. Its tough beak can slice up fish and crack the shells of crabs. Softshells also enjoy munching on the flowers of water plants.

SOFTSHELL TURTLE

Turtles are weird-looking creatures, but the softshell turtles are the weirdest of the lot. While other turtles are slow beasts that haul a tough protective case around with them, softshells, as their name suggests, do not. Instead, they have given up some protection to gain more speed and become fast-moving, stealthy killers. Their rubber shells and funny trunk-like snouts might make them seem cute, but you need to watch out when there's a softshell about: they bite for defence, giving humans a very deep cut.

SOFTSHELL TURTLE
TRIONYCHIDAE FAMILY
Lifespan: 20 years
Size: 27–100 cm (11–39 in)

GLOBAL FAMILY
Softshell turtles live in lakes and rivers all over the world (except Australia) – wherever it is nice and warm. There are 25 species in all, with the biggest one living in the Yangtze River in China.

AIR IN WATER
Softshells do not need to come to the surface to breathe. They wriggle their lips to pump water through their mouths, and oxygen in the water passes through their gums into the blood.

THE NAMIB'S WEIRD LIZARDS

It does not rain much in the Namib, but moisture arrives as fog rolling in from the sea. The web-footed dune gecko climbs to the top of dunes to catch the fog. Its webbed feet stop it sinking in the sand. Tiny water droplets form on the gecko's smooth skin and the lizard then licks up the moisture.

The Namaqualand chameleon changes the colour of its skin to match the conditions. In the cool morning, it goes black to absorb warmth from the sunshine. By midday, it has turned pale to reflect away extra heat and blend in with the sand. When necessary, it is dark on one side and pale on the other!

Running over loose sand is very hard work. The shovel-snouted lizard whirls its back legs like paddlewheels to push itself faster than any other desert reptile. When resting, the lizard always holds two feet off the ground, dancing between each pair to stop its feet burning on the hot sand. When it gets too hot on the surface, the lizard uses its curved snout to dig deep under the cool sand.

NAMIB WEB-FOOTED DUNE GECKO

The Namib is one of the strangest places on Earth. This vast desert runs along the coast of south-west Africa, where the strong sea breezes blow the red sand into colossal sand dunes – some of which are the tallest in the world. Three lizards living in the Namib's vast ocean of sand use some unique tricks to stay alive: The web-footed dune gecko drinks the air, the Namaqua chameleon uses solar power, while the shovel-snouted lizard can swim through sand!

NAMIB WEB-FOOTED DUNE GECKO
PACHYDACTYLUS RANGEI
Lifespan: 5 years
Size: 13 cm (5 in)

ANCIENT LAND
The Namib is the oldest desert on Earth. It has been a dry wasteland for 80 million years – since before the dinosaurs died out.

UP PERISCOPE
The peringuey adder also lives in the Namib. It has eyes right on top of its head, so it can look up for prey while almost completely buried under the sand.

MORE WEIRD REPTILES

Leaf-nosed snake

This slender tree snake from Madagascar is like a living twig. The females even have a leaf-shaped snout, which is used to signal to mates. The snake ambushes lizards in the trees, and when resting, it just hangs down from a branch.

Egg-eating snake

These little snakes do not need strong venom or great strength. They slide silently into a bird's nest and swallow an egg whole – shell and all. The stomach juices burn through the shell so it eventually cracks and the snake can digest the little chick inside.

Spiderman lizard

The Mwanza flat-headed rock agama from East Africa has a much more fun name: the Spiderman lizard. It has a red head and back and blue legs, so it looks like it's wearing the superhero's outfit. However, it does not fire a net of sticky silk like Spidey – when it meets a rival lizard, the two just bash each other with their tails.

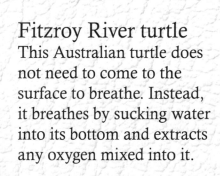

Fitzroy River turtle

This Australian turtle does not need to come to the surface to breathe. Instead, it breathes by sucking water into its bottom and extracts any oxygen mixed into it.

Big-headed turtle

This Chinese turtle's head is too big to fit under its shell. So the bighead has come up with another way to stay safe. It wears a helmet of bone that covers the top and side of the head.

WEIRD DINOSAURS

Therizinosaurus

Standing on its back legs, this weird dinosaur was more than 4 m (13 ft) tall. It was covered in feathers, and had claws that were 1 metre (39 in) long – the longest of any animal. When the first fossils were unearthed in the 1940s, scientists thought the claws must be horns. However, now it is thought that the long claws were for hooking on to tree branches and pulling them down to the dinosaur's mouth.

Microraptor

Birds evolved from dinosaurs, and experts think that this small dinosaur was able to fly. However, it was not a bird, nor some kind of early relative of birds. The big giveaway is that *Microraptor* had not two but four wings. The pair on its back legs had long flight feathers. The wings enabled it at least to glide down from trees or cliffs, but some experts think *Microraptor* was a powerful flier.

Linhenykus monodactylus

This small, agile dinosaur had long back legs for running fast. The same cannot be said about its forelegs, which were reduced to just a single finger bone each. It is assumed that these fingers did nothing at all.

Parasaurolophus

This dinosaur had a mouth like a duck's bill and a large crest arcing back from its head. The beak-shaped mouth was for grazing on tough water plants. The reason for the crest is less well understood. It might have been used in fights or perhaps to make the dino's calls sound louder.

GLOSSARY

absorb
to take in a gas or liquid through a surface. Many reptiles absorb water or oxygen through their skin

aggressive
to be willing to fight other animals

animal kingdom
the group of life-forms that contains all animals. Life on Earth is divided into at least five kingdoms: animals, plants, fungi, protists (tiny creatures) and bacteria (germs)

clones
animals that have exactly the same genes as each other. Twins are a kind of clone

dingo
a wild dog that lives in Australia. Dingos are descended from pet dogs introduced to Australia by human settlers about 3,500 years ago

exotic
describing a plant or animal that comes from another part of the world

genes
the instructions used to build a living body. The instructions used by a life-form come from their parents – or parent

insects
a very common and varied group of animals that have six legs and bodies arranged in three sections

marine
to do with the ocean

newt
a relative of frogs that has four legs and a tail. It looks like a reptile but is an amphibian

parthenogenesis
the process in which babies are produced inside a mother without the need for a father

sand dunes
tall hills made from sand. Dunes are formed by the wind blowing sand into huge heaps

unique
one of a kind, unlike anything else

webbed feet
feet that have flaps of skin between the toes. Webbing makes the foot much larger; animals use webbed feet for swimming and flying

INDEX

The Author

Tom Jackson has written about 200 books over 25 years – his specialties are natural history, technology and all things scientific. Tom studied zoology at Bristol University and has worked in zoos and as a conservationist. He's mucked out polar bears, surveyed Vietnamese jungle and rescued wildlife from drought in Africa. Writing jobs have also taken him to the Galápagos Islands, the Amazon rainforest and the Sahara. Today, Tom lives in Bristol, England, with his wife and three children, and can be found mostly in the attic.

The Illustrator

Paul Collicutt is based in Brighton, England, and has worked as an author and illustrator for clients around the world. He created the *Robot City* project for Templar Publishing and has illustrated graphic novels and children's books. He won the Parents' Choice Gold Award in the USA for his picture book *This Train*. As a child, Paul lived in Kenya and is still scared of the possibility of meeting crocodiles!

Picture Credits (abbreviations: t = top; b = bottom; c = centre; l = left; r = right)
© www.shutterstock.com:

1 c, 2 cl, 3 c, 4 c, 5 b, 6 tl, 6 bc, 7 t, 7 bc, 9 c, 13 c, 15 c, 17 c, 19 c, 21 c, 23 c, 25 c, 27 c, 29 tr, 29 br, 32 r.

11 c Chris Mattison / Alamy Stock Photo

28 t, 28 b, 29cl Wikimedia Commons